Paddington's 123

by Michael Bond

Illustrated by John Lobban

Devised by Carol Watson

PUFFIN BOOKS

Published by the Penguin Group
Penguin Books USA Inc., 375 Hudson Street, New York, New York 10014, U.S.A.
Penguin Books Canada Ltd, 10 Alcorn Avenue, Toronto, Ontario, Canada M4V 3B2

Penguin Books Ltd, Registered Offices: Harmondsworth, Middlesex, England

First published by William Collins Sons & Co. Ltd., 1990
First published in the United States of America by Viking,
a division of Penguin Books USA Inc., 1991
Published in Puffin Books, 1996

3 5 7 9 10 8 6 4

Text copyright © Michael Bond, 1990
Illustrations copyright © William Collins Sons & Co. Ltd., 1990
All rights reserved

Puffin Books ISBN 0-14-055762-8

1

One Paddington Bear

2

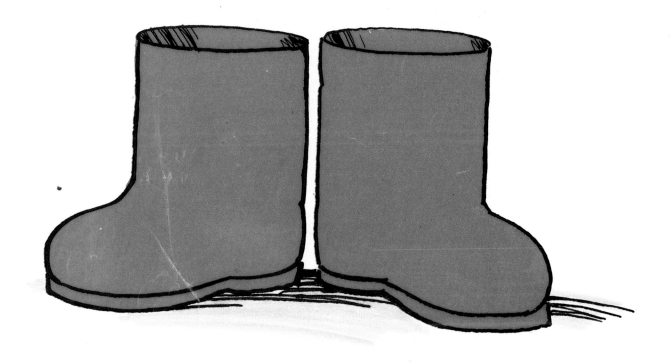

two boots

3

three suitcases

4

four buttons

5

five ice cream
sundaes

6

six hats

7

seven mugs

8

eight candles

9

nine postcards

10

ten buckets

11

eleven shovels

12

twelve flags

13

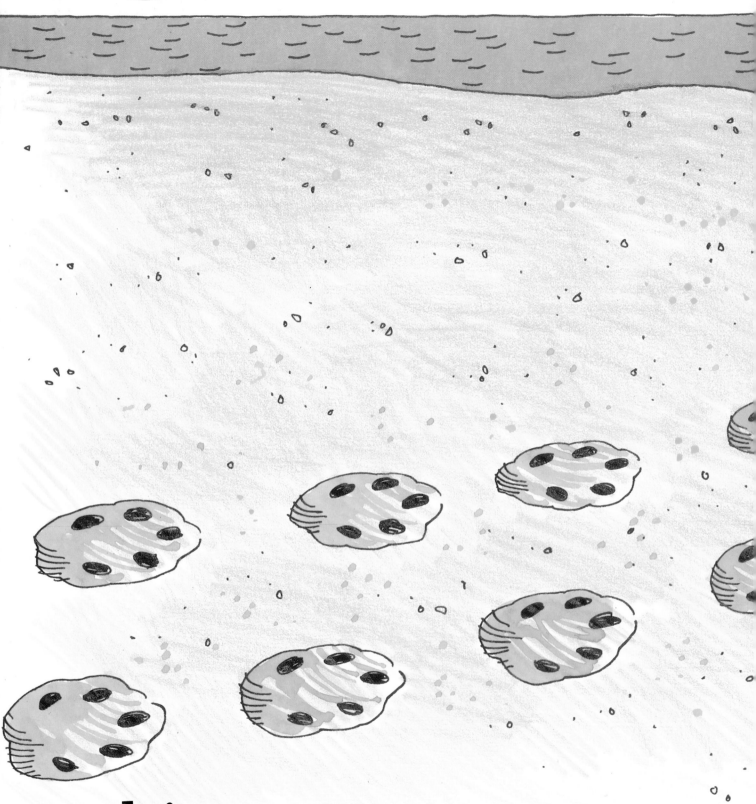

thirteen pawprints

14

fourteen balloons

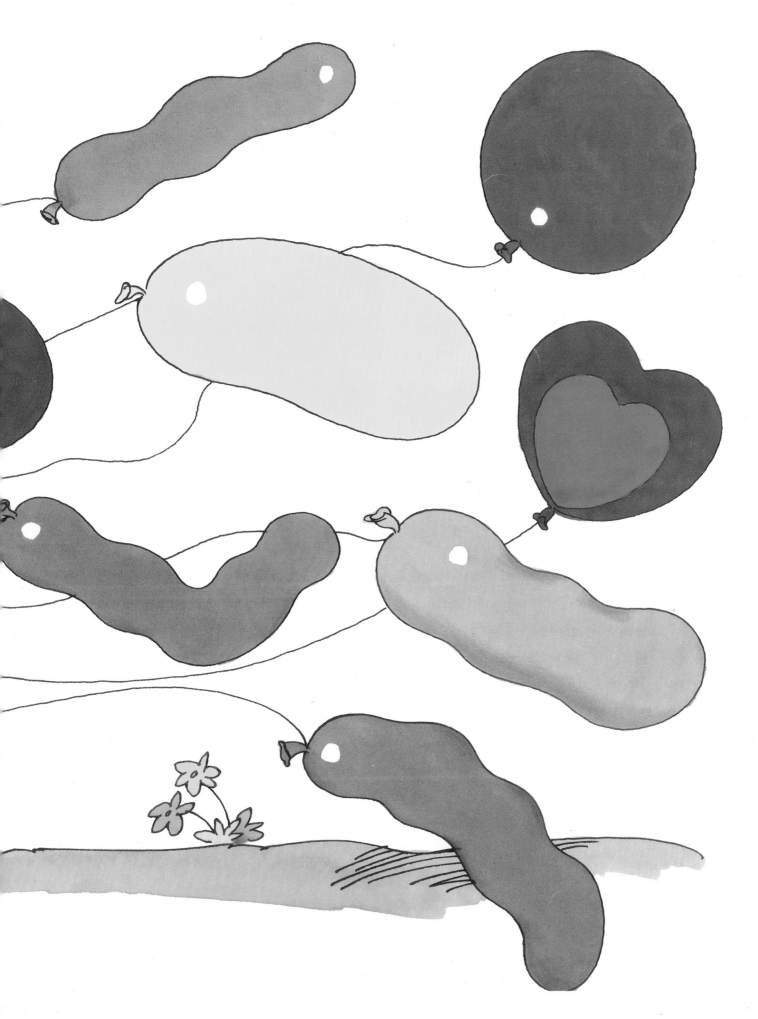

15

fifteen jars of
marmalade

16

sixteen crayons

17

seventeen jam tarts

18

eighteen stars

19

nineteen fish

twenty marmalade sandwiches

Now there are only 19 sandwiches left!
Can you find them hidden in this
picture?

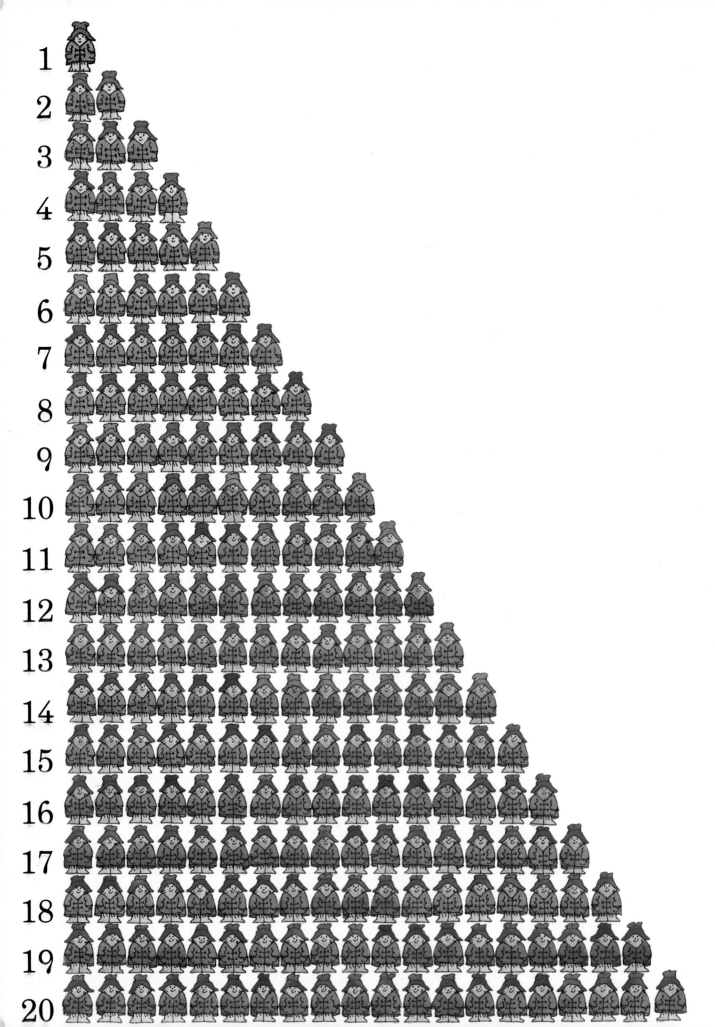

1
2
3
4
5
6
7
8
9
10
11
12
13
14
15
16
17
18
19
20